Instituto Plinio Corrêa de Oliveira

The Most Monumental Social Engineering and Ideological Transshipment Effort in History

Is Bolstered by Mass Hysteria and Vatican Support

São Paulo, 2020

Table of Contents

Foreword

Following in the footsteps of the illustrious Catholic thinker whose name it bears, the Plinio Corrêa de Oliveira Institute (IPCO), based in São Paulo, Brazil, defends the ideals of Tradition, Family and Property in this Latin American country.

Concerned with the ideological manipulation of the coronavirus crisis in an anti-Christian sense, the IPCO has recently published two documents of great doctrinal significance.

The first is titled "Warning! A Virus Threatens the Future of Brazil and Christian Civilization! - The Catholic Concept of the Common Good Is the Antidote to the Pandemic's Ideological Manipulation

The second, which we are publishing in full below, is titled "The Most Monumental Social Engineering and Ideological Transshipment Effort in History Is Bolstered by Mass Hysteria and Vatican Support."

This document denounces governments that have taken drastic confinement measures with enormous social and economic costs based on uncertain data and questionable mathematical models. No society can preserve public health for a long time at the expense of economic health.

Who benefits from this crime? According to the IPCO, geopolitically speaking, the Chinese Communist regime will be the primary beneficiary of the crisis generated by the Wuhan epidemic. In Western societies, however, three ideological currents stand to benefit the most: environmentalists, promoters of global governance, and the radical left. All three unanimously proclaim that "nothing will ever be the same again!"

This ideological shift, which has led people to submit to the severe restrictions on freedom and to accept with resignation the advent of a "new world," is encouraged not only by panic but also by promises of financial aid from the welfare state. This manipulation of opinion closely resembles the one Plinio Corrêa de Oliveira analyzed in his 1965 essay titled Unperceived Ideological Transshipment and Dialogue, the Latest Communist Ploy to Conquer World Opinion.

The IPCO document concludes by accusing the Vatican of having contributed to boosting the climate of general panic and fostering an attitude of sympathy for the emerging "new normality."

As shown by Pope Francis' support for the so-called "popular" movements in Latin America and his repeated calls for integral ecology and a new model of globalization, the Catholic hierarchy has indeed given its blessing in advance to the most monumental social engineering effort in history.

Preamble

If the *Guinness Book of Records* were to track the most senseless attitude possible, the award would probably go to someone who committed suicide for fear of dying.

With the coronavirus epidemic, that is what the world is doing. It is playing out on the social scale, the very same chain reaction the SARS-CoV-2 virus[*] triggers in its victims: An overreaction by the body's immune system leads to blockage in the lungs and death by asphyxiation.

---

[*]Throughout this document, except for quotes from other sources, we will employ the correct technical terms. Thus, SARS-CoV-2 designates the virus currently in circulation, and COVID-19 the disease it causes.

Apocalyptic Projections Based on Unreliable Mathematical Models

We can exemplify with Italy, the first Western nation attacked by the virus originating in China.

The World Health Organization (WHO) initially minimized the virus's outbreak in Wuhan and congratulated the Chinese communist regime on its work to contain the epidemic. On February 17, however, through the Italian-American scientist Ira Longini, an important consultant, the WHO reversed itself. Based on statistical data provided by the Chinese leadership, it estimated that the virus would infect 66% of the planet's 7.7 billion inhabitants, causing the death of 45 – 50 million people.

Transferring these projections to Italy, journalist Alberto Rossi calculated that if the country had not been more agile than others in isolating involuntary virus spreaders, the number of infected Italians would be in the 36 – 40 million range. He estimated the death toll would reach 400 – 450 thousand, equivalent to Italy's dead during the Second World War: 330,000 soldiers and 130,000 civilians.[1]

Other journalists made even more apocalyptic calculations: "Suppose that in the end, only 30% are infected, close to 20 million" – imagined Francesco Sisci in the daily *Il Sussidiario* of March 9. "If – giving a discount – 10% of them go into a [respiratory] crisis, that means that without intensive care therapy, they are bound to succumb. There would be two million direct deaths, plus all indirect ones resulting from a collapse of the health system."[2]

A week later, Imperial College London released a team study led by Prof. Neil Ferguson. It became the pretext for many governments to impose extreme stay-at-home measures. The model predicted that, in the absence of such shelter-in-place orders, there would be approximately 510,000 deaths in the United Kingdom and 2.2 million in the United States, as it was a virus "with comparable lethality to H1N1 influenza in 1918 [the Spanish flu]."[3] This was shocking information, but presumably exaggerated, one would think. A 2005 reconstruction of the Spanish flu virus carried out at the Centers for Disease Control in Atlanta, as well as subsequent studies, showed that the Spanish flu was a hundred times more lethal than other forms of influenza seen in the twentieth century.[4]

Although initial information coming from Wuhan did not corroborate this claim about the virus's extreme lethality, the Imperial College's projections were taken almost as a "dogma of faith." They led the British government to change its policy. The latter did not lift stay-at-home measures even when Prof. Ferguson, acknowledged in a tweet: "I'm conscious that lots of people would like to see and run the pandemic simulation code we are using to model control measures against COVID-19. To explain the background – *I wrote the code (thousands of lines of undocumented C) 13+ years ago* to model flu pandemics."[5]

The revelation provoked hundreds of Twitter responses, pointing to the extreme vulnerability of this programming language, further weakened by its large number of undocumented lines, which make independent verification almost impossible.[6] Ten days later, a University of Oxford team came up with an alternative model assuming that a much larger number of inhabitants of the British Isles would already be contaminated so that the lethality rate would be far lower.[7]

Time will tell which model will prove to be more accurate. In any case, an April 9 study issued by the Institute of Virology at the University of Bonn presented a factual confirmation of the Oxford model. It denied the lethality rate that WHO and the Imperial College attributed to SARS-CoV-2. The study consisted of several in-depth tests carried out on people from the village of Gangelt, in the district of Heinsberg, the epidemic's first focus in Germany. The daily *Le Monde* summarizes its results as follows: "A German study estimates a lower mortality rate. Surveys of 12,446 Gangelt residents show figures five times less than the original assessment. The researchers argue that this method identifies all infected people, including asymptomatic carriers."

The study found that the population had a 15% infection rate, and the mortality rate was only 0.37%, which is five times lower than that assigned to Germany by John Hopkins University.[8]

In any case, it does not seem sensible for governments to take drastic measures, with enormous social and economic costs, based on mathematical models built on uncertain data. To prove it, let's look again at Italy.

On the day these lines are written (April 20, 2020), the Civil Protection bulletin announced that, for the first time since the beginning of the crisis, both the number of people testing positive in the country and those in intensive care units in need of respiratory help had decreased. One can thus assume that the peak of the epidemic is behind us (except that the virus can mutate and cause a new epidemic wave, as happened with the H1N1 swine flu virus between 2009 and 2011).[9]

To date, Italy's official death toll from COVID-19 is 23,660. Suppose that the virus does not mutate, and that number will double by the end of the year. The total number of deaths would amount to 47,000. That would be almost *ten times fewer deaths* than the least alarmist projection made at the beginning of the epidemic, and *fifty times less* than the most alarmist projection made a mere month ago.

Forty thousand deaths is a very high toll. It would be a tragedy for the victims and their families, and a severe blow to Italy. Nor would that tragedy be lessened by the fact that the average age for the deceased is 81 years old (mostly males) with pre-existing pathologies in two-thirds of the cases, according to data provided by Italy's *Istituto Superiore de Sanitá*.[10]

Economic Consequences "of Biblical Proportions," Visible to the Naked Eye

Now let us look at the medal's flip side: The economic consequences resulting from the drastic "horizontal" stay-at-home measures adopted in a short period by Italy's national and regional authorities to contain the epidemic and the overwhelming of hospitals' ICUs.

According to the Italian Institute of Statistics, 2.2 million companies suspended their activities, 49% of the total. That led to a 34% production drop and a 27% added value drop. A total of 7.4 million employees were unable to work (44.3% of the entire workforce), of whom 4.9 million were simple wage earners (42%).[11]

This sudden halt in economic activity will lead to "a tragedy of biblical proportions," predicts Mario Draghi, former president of the European Central Bank in a column in the *Financial Times*. It is the biggest crisis in the real economy in the last hundred years. According to investment bank Goldman Sachs, Italian GDP will fall 11.6% in 2020.[12] For Gustavo Boni, a European official, the contraction of Italian GDP will be between 12.5% and 15%, with an 85% drop in gross fixed capital stock and a 38% drop in domestic employment income. In turn, public debt will amount to 160% of GDP. That was Greece's level when it was bailed out by the EU.[13]

Added up, this means that, once stay-at-home orders are lifted, millions of Italian workers risk finding their companies' doors locked, and thousands of artisans and retailers could join the large numbers of the unemployed or file for bankruptcy. In the tourism sector alone (13% of Italian GDP), the economic newspaper *Il Sole 24 Ore* calculates that "almost one million jobs are at risk."[14]

Maurizio Gardini, president of Confcooperative, one of the main associations of Italian cooperatives, says that when Italy lifts the shutdown, at least 20% (close to one million) of medium and small companies will be dead in the water. The consequences in terms of lost income, unemployment, and social unrest are indescribable.[15] A study by the Italian statistics agency (ISTAT) holds that the lockdown of productive activities will generate "the collapse of consumer and business confidence."[16]

Italy is not an isolated case. Authorities in neighboring France have taken similar shutdown measures, based on equally alarmist projections of contagion and deaths. The consequences are similar as well. According to INSEE, the French statistics institute, economic activity fell 36%, while in the private sector, the drop was even greater (42%). In fact, 6.9 million private-sector employees are at home receiving partial unemployment assistance, and household consumption dropped by 35%.[17]

The economist and historian Nicolas Baverez said in his weekly column in the daily *Le Figaro* that "two months of confinement will leave France with a 10% drop in its GDP, a deficit of 12% to 15% and a public debt of more than 120% of GDP. Thousands of companies will go bankrupt, notably the smallest ones, and many of the 8.7 million partially unemployed will never get their jobs back, resulting in the growth of poverty."[18] (In fact, the Minister of Labor announced that 9.6 million private-sector employees are currently "protected" by partial unemployment benefits. That is almost half of the entire labor force).[19]

According to Bruno Le Maire, French Economy Minister, in 2020, the country will experience its biggest recession since World War II.[20] Prime Minister Edouard Philippe declared in the National Assembly that the economic impact linked to the coronavirus will be "massive" and "brutal," giving rise to "an economic shock that everyone imagines, but whose total impact no one yet knows."[21]

If these are the forecasts for two countries whose economies are among the world's most developed, one can only imagine what will be the impact from the SARS-CoV-2 blocking of economic activities for the rest of the world.

The Devastating Social Impact of the "Great Shutdown": the Pandemic of Extreme Poverty

On April 9, Kristalina Georgieva, Managing Director of the International Monetary Fund, declared we would see "the worst economic consequences since the Great Depression" of 1929, causing a drop in income per inhabitant in over 179 countries. The senior official added that poor or emerging countries in Africa, Asia, and Latin America "are at high risk," all the more so as capital is migrating out of them at a rate three times faster than the 2008 financial crisis, which will trigger liquidity and solvency problems.[22]

Just five days later, the I.M.F. released its forecasts regarding what it called "the Great Shutdown": a contraction of 3% of world GDP in 2020, with Europe and the United States being the most affected by the depression (-7.5% and -6.5% respectively). It does not rule out the possibility of an even more brutal drop in 2021. The social effect of the recession will be severe, with unemployment in the Eurozone increasing by 40% (reaching 9.2%) and tripling in the U.S.A. to reach 10.4% of the total workforce.[23]

"Workers and businesses are facing catastrophe," stated Guy Ryder, Director-General of the International Labor Organization. The I.L.O. did indeed release an April 7 report, saying that "the crisis is causing an unprecedented reduction in economic activity and working time. As of 1 April 2020, estimates indicate that working hours will decline in the current quarter (Q2) by around 6.7 percent, which is equivalent to 195 million full-time workers."[24]

Huge losses are expected at all income levels but especially in high to middle-income countries (7% loss, equivalent to 100 million full-time workers), which is much greater than the effects of the 2008 financial crisis. The sectors most affected will be hotels, restaurants, manufacturing, retailing, administrative activities, and services. The ILO report states that there is a high risk that the final figure will be much higher than the initial projection of 25 million unemployed.[25]

This figure of 25 million certainly was extremely optimistic, since a study by the African Union suggested that Africa alone would see the suppression of 20 million jobs, and indebtedness would escalate.[26] As far as the United States is concerned, it went from almost full employment in February "to mass unemployment expected to reach 20% in April. In less than a month, 22 million jobs have disappeared," says the *Figaro*'s Washington correspondent.[27]

The global result will be an exponential increase in extreme poverty. "I see no historical equivalent to the threat that COVID-19 poses to the most vulnerable populations," said Robin Guittard, Oxfam campaign manager in France.[28] In a study released on April 8, researchers at King's College London and the National University of Australia predict that the pandemic could bring extreme poverty to half a billion of the planet's inhabitants, destroying the progress made in the past three decades.[29]

The Increase in Deaths From Hunger in Poor Countries Will Be Much Greater Than That of COVID-19 Victims

The consequences of this exponential increase in poverty on the health of impoverished populations will be disastrous. Even the World Health Organization, the biggest promoter of strict stay-at-home measures, recognizes that there is a close link between extreme poverty and poor health. In a study published in conjunction with the Organisation for Economic Co-operation and Development, it recognizes the obvious, namely, that "The poor suffer worse health and die younger. They have higher than the average child and maternal mortality, higher levels of disease, and more limited access to health care and social protection."[30]

Consequently, more than 3.42 million people died of hunger in the first months of 2020, a daily average of 30,800 deaths. That is, *almost five times more* than the global number of deaths by COVID-19 on April 5, the day registering the highest number of fatalities (6,367 victims) worldwide so far.

The World Food Program predicts that the loss of tourism revenues, the decrease in remittances and travel and other restrictions related to the coronavirus pandemic will double the number of poor people suffering from acute hunger, adding 130 million to the approximately 135 million already existing in that category. "'COVID-19 is potentially catastrophic for millions who are already hanging by a thread,' said Arif Husain, chief economist and director of research, assessment, and monitoring at the World Food Programme (WFP)."[31] David Beasly, WFP Executive Director, exclaimed in an interview with *The Guardian*: "Now, my goodness, this is a perfect storm. We are looking at widespread famines of biblical proportions."[32]

Statistically, this increase in acute hunger resulting from the economic collapse caused by confinement measures could be responsible for 30,000 additional daily deaths. A sizable share of those deaths would probably have been avoided if instead of listening to WHO ayatollahs and media icons, the authorities had listened to the opinions of other experts who suggested vertical isolation or *smart* virus control measures. In so doing, they would protect the population at risk (the elderly and people with serious underlying diseases) and quarantining those infected by the virus after carrying out thousands of tests.[33]

This is not an unrealistic alternative. This plan was highly successful in Taiwan, South Korea, Singapore, Canada, Georgia, and Iceland.[34] In the first three Asian countries mentioned and in Japan, work stoppages affected only 10% of the active population.[35] The effectiveness of this strategy so far has been largely demonstrated. The total number of deaths in these four countries, with a combined population of 257.4 million people, today amounts to only 489, which corresponds to a mortality rate of 1.9 victims per million. In contrast, in Italy, despite the horizontal insulation strategy followed, where the entire population was ordered to stay at home, the figure was 391.32 victims per million (23,660 deceased), that is, 205 times more!

A March 19 editorial in *The Wall Street Journal* put it well, three days after the release of the Imperial College's fantasy projections and even before the Oxford University report. It was titled "Rethinking the Coronavirus Shutdown: No Society Can Safeguard Public Health for Long at the Cost of Its Economic Health."[36]

It is a pity that neither this editorial nor the above figures were shown to government officials who, driven by the good intention of saving lives and advised by WHO directors and Imperial College researchers, decided to halt "non-essential" economic operations in their countries. The impact of this paralysis will be all the more acute as "isolation, even if intermittent, should go on until 2022 in several parts of the world if a vaccine does not appear," according to the magazine *Isto é*, referencing "a study by Harvard University, published in the journal *Science*."[37]

In the Name of "Social Distancing," WHO Sacrifices Children in Poor Countries

In this hasty decision to order everyone to stay at home, there is yet another shocking revelation.

On March 26, the World Health Organization published a document titled "Guiding principles for immunization activities during the COVID-19 pandemic." It states that, based on "the recommended prevention measures of physical distancing, it is advised to *temporarily suspend the conduct of mass vaccination campaigns* due to the increased risk of promoting community circulation."[38]

Following this recommendation, the Global Polio Eradication Initiative has suspended its vaccination campaign. However, its scientific advisers estimate that this will increase the number of paralysis in children and that some countries free from this infectious disease will become infected again. According to the

Madrid daily *El País,* polio is just one of many vaccinations that have been suspended in Africa. "Writing in *Science,* journalist Leslie Roberts documents that *millions of children have been deprived of their polio, measles, papilloma, yellow fever, cholera, and meningitis vaccines.* There is talk of 14 million, but it is a low estimate, certainly very low."[39]

According to Atlanta's Centers for Disease Control, 23 countries have already stopped their measles campaigns, and another 16 are considering doing so even though it kills 3% to 6% of those infected (multiples more than COVID-19), and that the majority of its victims are malnourished children.

Facing what the Spanish newspaper calls the "devil's dilemma," authorities in most rich countries have chosen, like it or not, to spare potential COVID-19 victims (perhaps because they are a majority of voters) and to sacrifice children in poor countries. These will die or become disabled because of WHO's irresponsible guidance.[40]

Given these data, would the reader not agree with us that the contemporary world is committing suicide for fear of dying from

COVID-19? That is happening thanks to the irresponsibility of the WHO, political leaders, and media, which created the ongoing hysteria.

That is so obvious that a question naturally surfaces: Who benefits from this collective suicide in our contemporary society?

The Four Main Beneficiaries of This Collective Suicide

From a geopolitical point of view, the major beneficiary of the crisis generated by the epidemic that started in Wuhan was China's Communist regime itself. But, within Western societies, three ideological currents (all of which, by the way, have shown themselves to be the great champions of extreme stay-at-home measures) will be its main beneficiaries: radical ecologists, world governance advocates, and the radical left.

1. THE COMMUNIST PARTY OF CHINA

Despite the huge responsibility of China's communist rulers for the still unclarified origins of the SARS-CoV-2 virus and its spread in Wuhan and the entire Hubei province,[41] its greatest beneficiary, both internally and externally, is undoubtedly the communist regime in Beijing. John Gray, professor emeritus at the London School of Economics, summarizes it in an article for the *NewStatesman*:

No one knows the full human costs of the Chinese shutdown. Even so, Xi Jinping's regime looks to have benefited from the pandemic. The virus has provided a rationale for expanding the surveillance state and introducing even stronger political control. Instead of wasting the crisis, Xi is using it to expand the country's influence. China is inserting itself in place of the EU by assisting distressed national governments, such as Italy. Many of the masks and testing kits it has supplied have proved to be faulty, but the fact seems not to have dented Beijing's propaganda campaign. . . .

The Serbian president Aleksandar Vucic has been blunter and more realistic: "European solidarity does not exist . . . that was a fairy tale. The only country that can help us in this hard situation is the People's Republic of China. To the rest of them, thanks for nothing."[42]

Bolivarian left-wing currents support this diplomatic and ideological expansion of Chinese influence. For example, Brazilian activist Paola Estrada, a member of Secretariat of the International Peoples Assembly, and also of the Brazilian chapter of ALBA Movements (Continental Coordination of Social Movements toward the Bolivarian Alliance for the Peoples of Our America). She attests:

> It is becoming increasingly obvious that during the pandemic, China has taken on a much more prominent role than before in the economic and commercial spheres, as well as in the political and ideological aspects. It is still difficult to project scenarios for the outcome of this process. However, it is undeniable that the Chinese government has been applauded worldwide for its capacity, effectiveness, and speed in facing the advance of the epidemic in China. They did so by enforcing measures of social isolation, building hospitals, manufacturing tests and hospital supplies, qualifying professionals, and investing in science and technology. . . . In times of pandemic, when we have to deal with so many changes, uncertainties, sadness, and attacks by the right and imperialism, the example of the Venezuelan people, the

2. ECOLOGISTS

Soon after governments implemented stay at home measures, ecologists shouted loud and clear that it had been proven that in the face of a global threat, it was possible to impose drastic measures affecting the daily life of whole populations.[44] They suggested that, once the health crisis is over, it would be illogical not to declare a *climate emergency* and impose equally drastic measures to decrease CO_2 production.[45]

In Spain, five associations (Amigos de la Tierra, Greenpeace, Ecologistas en Acción, SEO/BirdLife, and WWF) addressed the European Commission and the Spanish government. They requested that the relief and stimulus packages meant to reactivate the economy be used to "speed up the transition to a carbon-free and green economy." The distribution of funds should penalize "those most unsustainable activities" and be conditional on a commitment "to stop the loss of biodiversity" and favor "decarbonization."[46]

Furthermore, the "European Alliance for a Green Recovery" was born at the initiative of MEP Pascal Confin. It includes 180 European leaders (79 MEPs from 17 countries, 37 top managers of multinational corporations, 28 business associations, and seven NGOs, in addition to groups of experts). Its purpose is to promote a "green" solution to the coronavirus economic crisis and to "unleash a new European economic model." Since, for the Alliance, the "core element of economic strategy" must be "the fight against climate change," the "massive investments" to be made to save the economy must align with "ecological principles." The Alliance supports a letter that 13 European Union Environment and Climate Ministers sent to Brussels demanding that the Green Pact proposed by the newly empowered von der Leyen Commission be retained.[47]

3. GLOBALISTS

As soon as European countries began to close their borders and take protective measures, "open society" advocates started to proclaim that the only solution for the pandemic would be a coordinated global response. Meanwhile, the nations bickered among themselves over the defective masks and test kits that China had "generously" sent.

Bill Gates published in several newspapers a column titled "A Global Strategy Against COVID-19," saying that although governments have provided national responses, their leaders must recognize that as long as the virus is present somewhere, "it will be a problem for the entire world." He added that "we need a global response to fighting the disease" so that financial and medical resources (face masks, test kits, etc.) are distributed effectively, and countries commit to following WHO guidelines.[48]

For his part, Antônio Guterres, former president of the Socialist International and current UN secretary-general, presented a special report titled "Shared responsibility, global solidarity: Responding to the socio-economic impacts of COVID-19." In it, he asks that at least 10% of world GDP be allocated to a solidarity fund to resolve the crisis.[49]

Gordon Brown, a former British Labor Prime Minister, gave the last touch to the package by suggesting no less than some provisional form of global government to face the twin, medical and economic crises: "What we need is a working executive."[50] He is now acting as a UN special envoy for global education. And in an interview with *El País*, he reiterated:

> We need a [summit] with commitments to provide the health emergency with the necessary funds. . . . And secondly, an Executive Task Force [a team with executive powers] at the G20, because good words are no longer enough. We need to take action in the coming days and do so in a coordinated manner. An executive body is needed to respond to the problem that you [the journalist] mention on [criticism] of international institutions. . . . Shared political leadership is needed.

According to Brown, in the current phase of efforts to preserve jobs, a national response may suffice. Still, in the next phase,

> we will need fiscal coordination, monetary coordination, and collaboration between the different central banks. And I am not just talking about a model like the EU. I refer to the global scope. . . . In the growth phase, we will need a coordinated effort of fiscal stim-

ulus around the world.[51]

In Latin America, the so-called Puebla Group made up of presidents, former presidents (e.g., Lula da Silva, Dilma Rousseff, etc.) and socialist-oriented political, academic, and union leaders, published a statement. The signatories asserted that the current crisis "has no other solution than integrating Latin America and the Caribbean, and cooperating at the global level." In this operation, the statement continued, the WHO "must play an even more important role than today."

The document invited "governments, organizations, and peoples of the world, when the pandemic ends, to make a serene reflection on a New Development Model that prioritizes previously unknown values such as the environment, social inclusion, reducing inequality, food security, military disarmament, multilateralism, and fiscal progressivity."[52]

4. The Radical Left

In turn, the radical left is lying in wait to surf the wave. In an article published in *Intercept*, writer and activist Naomi Klein explained that in the last two decades, she learned that "During moments of cataclysmic change, the previously unthinkable suddenly becomes a reality." [53]

Along the same line, the Slovenian philosopher Slavoj Žižek maintained that "the coronavirus will force us to reinvent communism based on trust in people and science." It would not be like the communism of the past. Rather, it would be "some kind of global organization that can control and regulate the economy, as well as limit the sovereignty of nation-states." The Italian philosopher Franco Berardi Bifo would not be outdone: "Is there anyone who does not like this logic because it recalls communism? Well, if there are no more modern words, we will still use this one, old indeed, but always very beautiful."[54]

The radical left is acting coherently. It is openly proposing the nationalization of electric and telecommunications companies, private hospitals, hotels, etc. Pablo Iglesias, leader of the *Podemos* party and vice-president of the current Spanish coalition government, stated it eloquently during a meeting of his crisis cabinet.[55]

Even more troubling is the fact that representatives of the Establishment are taking up proposals made until now by the radical left, such as a "universal basic income." Note that the proposed monthly check from the government is not limited to temporary aid to unemployed workers due to economic or financial crisis. All sensible people, ranging from an analyst of the Acton Institute[56] to the secretary of the Spanish Bishops' Conference,[57] consider that necessary. Nor does universal basic income correspond to Milton Friedman's 'helicopter money' metaphor aimed at solving an economy's temporary liquidity problems.[58] In reality, it is a permanent minimum wage distributed to the entire population, each person being able to choose whether or not he wants to work. The measure would supposedly guarantee the individual's total "emancipation."

A "universal basic income" was the central plank in the platform of Benoît Hamon, the French Socialist Party's unsuccessful candidate for the presidency, in the recent elections. He took advantage of the epidemic to relaunch this proposal, claiming that "the universal wage for existence is an incomparable tool for emancipation. . . . Freeing everyone from exclusive dependence on salary earned at work, the universal wage gives each individual the ability to negotiate and choose. . . . Social emancipation goes through this individual practice of freedom. . . . The crisis will give birth to a new world."[59]

In an open letter published in the London newspaper *The Independent*, no fewer than 500 academics and political leaders, mainly from the United Kingdom and the United States, called for the implementation of this universal basic income. They stated that "Without drastic government intervention, countless numbers will suffer, businesses will close, unemployment will skyrocket, and the economy will go into a steep recession and possibly even a second Great Depression." Therefore, "an unconditional basic income should play a central role in the emergency response to this crisis."[60] However, as far as we are concerned, this cure is worse than the disease[61][**].

Beppe Grillo, the former comedian and

[**]Financial analyst Maurizio Milano made a lucid criticism of the "wartime socialism" that these academics and leaders advocate by calling for the creation, ex nihilo, of a huge mass of financial liquidity to acquire public and private debts, thus increasing deficits and the public debt: "Historical evidence teaches us that 'emergencies' are the ideal breeding ground for an increasingly invasive action by states, leading to irresponsible and fragile societies to the detriment of freedom, security, and general well-being."

founder of Italy's Five Star Movement, signed on to this open letter. In addressing the issue of universal basic income, he declared: "The emergency we are experiencing could favor a historic, revolutionary change that many always superficially considered as crazy, but which could change our future for the better."[62]

A "New World" Imposed by Law . . . or by Force!

S ome firebrands want to precipitate this revolutionary change in a violent way. For example, congressman Guillaume Larrivée, from the center-right party *Les Républicains* (of former President Sarkozy), wrote a column in the newspaper *L'Opinion*. He speculated that, in France, "the brutality of the economic and financial outbreak would fuel a *social revolt* based on a fertile ground of concerns and demands already very much alive (as shown by 'yellow vest protesters' and the challenge to retirement reform in the last two years). That would reopen the wounds of class and generational struggle, as well as territorial disputes in the 'French archipelago,' kindling fiery riots." The French parliamentarian concludes: "I write without exaggeration: *France would then be on the way to civil war*."[63]

A report by the Central Territorial Intelligence Service (the French equivalent of the FBI) confirmed the French congressman's pessimistic prediction. It warned of a risk of social upheaval at the end of the lockdown. "Confinement prevents manifestations of popular discontent, but the anger does not diminish, and the highly criticized crisis management fuels the protests," says the report. Intelligence officers fear the creation of "fight committees" in urban peripheries and action by sectors of the extreme left to foster a "transversality of the struggles" [spreading them across the population].[64]

Indeed, disturbances have already started. "A non-exhaustive list of episodes of urban violence recorded between April 12 and April 19 includes Le Havre, Évreux, Bordeaux, Villiers-sur-Marne, Mantes-la-Jolie, Chanteloup-les-Vignes, Villeneuve-la-Garenne, La Courneuve, Trappes, Grigny," informs *Le Figaro*. "Ambushes are methodically prepared . . . with the storage of projectiles, mortars, and barricades to make the 'buzz' on social media. They observe the reactivity of the police and the mobilized personnel. The objective is clear: To assert that this is their territory and that they control it, a veteran police officer from a "sensitive sector" explains to the newspaper. The police have only one certainty: At the slightest incident, immediately denounced as a "police abuse," riots erupt, with multiple calls for reprisals on social networks, the Parisian newspaper adds.[65]

The situation could evolve rapidly from some early protests with controllable violence such as last year's "yellow vest" protests to massive and uncontrollable ones such as those in Santiago, Valparaíso, and other Chilean cities. These forced the government to yield to leftist pressure and to start a process that could result in the adoption of a Bolivarian-style constitution by a country that until recently boasted the highest per capita income in Latin America.

A Transitory "Window of Opportunity" That the Organizers of the "New World" do not Want to Miss

If this scenario worsens, the disturbances will serve as an argument to accelerate programs to socialize the economy through legal means. In any case, the three ideological currents mentioned above – ecologism, globalism, and radical left – are unanimous in affirming categorically: "Nothing will ever be the same again."

From where do the representatives of ideological currents with hitherto fringe importance at the ballot box derive so much self-assurance? Perhaps it stems from hopes that they will overcome their ongoing differences. Above all, though, they know they can rely on two factors that completely open up for them an unexpected "window of opportunity": The population's fear of the worsening or eventual second wave of the pandemic, and the moral support that Pope Francis has been giving to their agendas.

Panic Fueled by WHO, Governments, the Media, and Religious Authorities

In an online lecture, historian Roberto de Mattei recalled that contagion can be both a physical and psychological phenomenon. He recalled Gustave Le Bon, who wrote *The Crowd: A Study of the Popular Mind.* "The modern theory of contagion, which was inspired by Le Bon, explains how protected by the anonymity of a crowd the most calm individual can become aggressive, acting at the suggestion of others or in imitation of them. Panic is one of those feelings that is spread by social contagion, as happened during the French Revolution in the period called the Great Fear ['*Grande Peur*']."[66]

Jacques Attali, an advisor to all French presidents on both the left and right, from Mitterrand to Macron, seems to have understood very well the use of panic as a weapon to promote a political agenda such as laying the foundations for global governance. Shortly after the first alarms caused by the H1N1 virus, he wrote a May 3, 2009 article in the weekly *L'Express*. He stated: "History teaches us that *humanity does not evolve significantly until it is truly afraid*: it implements defense mechanisms sometimes intolerable (scapegoats and totalitarianisms); sometimes useful (distractions); sometimes effective (therapies, setting aside, if necessary, all previous moral principles). Then, after the crisis has passed, it transforms these mechanisms to make them compatible with individual freedom and inserts them into a democratic health policy. This beginning pandemic could boost one of those structuring fears."

The Élysée Palace's gray eminence imagined several scenarios for the epidemic and added that, better than any "humanitarian or ecological narrative," all of them could serve to "raise awareness of the need for altruism, at least in self-interest." And that, in any case, it would be necessary to "establish a world police, world stocks and, therefore, worldwide inspection. That way, one would arrive much faster than mere economic convenience would allow, *to lay the foundations of a true world government*." And he concluded: "Besides, it was through the hospital that seventeenth-century France began to establish a true State."[67]

At the moment, no data allows us to affirm that this plan is being implemented. But one thing is certain: Several factors have contributed to spreading panic and, whether willing or not, international and national public health organizations have lent themselves to amplify it.

Yahoo!Life reported on its interview with Dr. Iahn Gonsenhauser, the person responsible for patient safety at Ohio State University's Wexner Medical Center. "'We throw around the word pandemic – that terrifies people,' he says, noting the word can bring up the terrible historical pandemics such as the bubonic plague and smallpox. 'But really all we mean by that word is something that's spreading across a large geographic area in a short amount of time. But it doesn't necessarily indicate the virulence and deadliness of it. I think people think it's like the movie *Outbreak*.*** '"[68]

The doctor further explained that another factor that may be contributing to increasing the panic about the coronavirus in the northern hemisphere is that it occurred at the end of

---

*** The film "Outbreak" was a 1995 American medical disaster film directed by Wolfgang Petersen. It tells the story of a new virus that the American government kept secret for many years for eventual use as a biological weapon.

winter and shares similar symptoms with those of the seasonal flu. Many people affected by the latter thought they had contracted the coronavirus.

Interviewed by the Belgian daily *L'Echo*, the French agnostic philosopher André Comte-Sponville gave other reasons worth mentioning. He was asked why societies today are acting so differently from half a century ago when the Hong Kong flu killed some one million people. There was a general indifference to the death toll back then. He replied:

> The so-called 'Asian' flu of 1957 – 1958 had caused even more [deaths], and everyone forgot about it. Why this difference in treatment? I see three main reasons for this. First, globalization in its media aspect: We are informed in real-time of everything that is happening in the world. For example, every day, of the number of deaths in China or the United States, Italy, or Belgium. . . . Then, there is the novelty and the "cognitive bias" it causes: COVID-19 is a new disease, which, for this reason, causes even more worries and surprises. Finally, we try to ig-

> nore death, and it becomes even more unacceptable when we are reminded of it.[69]

The media turbocharged these psychological factors of propensity to fear. Under the pretext of inciting the population to observe the preventive safeguards suggested by the authorities, media outlets contributed to the panic through nonstop reporting with apocalyptic tones.

A striking example of this tendency to exaggerate is an April 4 BBC report titled "Coronavirus: Five-year-old Among Latest UK Victims," with daily information provided by the Ministry of Health. While the title highlights something that would fit in a single line of this report, which carries all kinds of news, the fact that the latter acknowledges that the girl suffered from an "underlying health condition" shows the title's alarmist bias.[70]

Le Figaro's columnist Renaud Girard denounced the tortuous nature of that news item: "While factually correct, the BBC article unconsciously feeds the collective psychosis by passing on this subliminal message: Even children die [from COVID-19]. Now, the statistical data shows just the opposite: The virus is almost harmless for children. Later, sociologists will have to carefully analyze the role that the media played in the emergence of a worldwide psychosis in the face of a less lethal disease."[71]

Religious authorities, in particular the Catholic hierarchy, was another social group that contributed to the mass hysteria. In applying restrictive measures, they often anticipated civil authorities or went beyond what these required. The worst possible example came from the Vicar of Rome, the center of Catholicism. After consulting Pope Francis, he closed all churches. "Access to the parish and non-parish churches of the Diocese of Rome open to the public, and to church buildings of any kind open to the public, is denied to all the faithful," decreed Angelo Cardinal De Donatis.[72] He had to reverse the order two days later, given the faithful's anger. However, being deprived of the sacraments and spiritual consolation that prayer provides in the interior of a church could only increase anguish in the face of the epidemic and, indirectly, induce panic.

Aware of this, when the government first imposed restrictions, and some French bishops went further than the authorities by forbidding

the celebration of masses and the administra-
tion of the sacraments, the Bishop of Bellay-Ars,
Most Rev. Pascal Roland, broke ranks with
them. He published a note titled "Coronavirus
Epidemic or Epidemic of Fear?" In it, he stated
that "more than the coronavirus epidemic, we
should fear the epidemic of fear," and that he
refused to "give in to collective panic and submit to the precautionary principle that seems
to move civil institutions." For the fearless prelate, "the collective panic that we are witnessing
today" was revealing of our "falsified relationship with the reality of death" and the "anxi-
ety-generating effects of the loss of God." And
he asked: "Why should we suddenly focus our
attention solely on the coronavirus? Why forget
that every year, the seasonal, banal flu affects
between two and six million patients in France
and causes approximately 8,000 deaths?" The
bishop concluded with an appeal: "So, let us
not give in to the fear epidemic! Let us not be
living-dead!"[73]

This communiqué, which in hindsight
appears so realistic and clear-sighted, became
a casualty to fear (and pressure from single is-
sue-obsessed media). It was removed from the
diocesan website.

Panic Has Led the Population to Submit to the Authorities' Stay at Home Orders Voluntarily

In Brazil and some parts of the United States, people have taken to the streets to protest stay at home orders. In Europe, however, panic has so far led the population to take a submissive attitude to the severe restrictions on freedom of movement imposed by the authorities.

In France, a rebellious country usually, the day after the announcement of the stay at home order issued by President Emmanuel Macron, 96% of those consulted approved of them, and 85% regretted they were not imposed earlier! Those were poll results despite the population's perfect awareness of the financial cost inherent to compliance.[74] The same is true in Spain, where a poll requested by *El País* revealed that only 21.9 percent believed that "we should make the stay at home order more flexible to reactivate the economy as soon as possible, even if this means a greater spread of the coronavirus." In comparison, 59.3 percent of those polled maintained that "the stay at home order should be maintained as long as possible, even if this means greater economic fallout and more unemployment."[75] In their opinion, the impact on the economy would be negative and lasting worldwide (61.1%), for Spain (69.7%), and the individual families of those surveyed (31%).

Under the headline "In Rich Countries, Health Remains the Priority," *Le Figaro* reported: "[A]ccording to a Kantar survey conducted between April 9 and 13 in Canada, France, Germany, Italy, Japan, and the United States, 37 percent of the population lost part of their income, and 16 percent had it cut in half. However, a large majority of those polled continue to approve the costly measures adopted to fight the virus." [76]

Even more serious, panic favors the population's likely acceptance of the blackmail being proposed to it to lift the stay at home order: Submit to government control through smartphone apps that will report if individuals have been in contact with anyone infected with the coronavirus.

A survey conducted in France by a team from the Oxford University School of Economics revealed that about 80% of the people questioned (1,000 smartphone owners) would undoubtedly or probably install such an app if available. Most would even agree that telephone companies automatically install the app on their customers' smartphones (with an option for customer uninstalling), and two-thirds of those questioned said they would probably or undoubtedly retain the vendor-installed app.

Approval for this blackmail (controlled "freedom of movement") is such that up to 40% of the interviewees would have a more favorable opinion of the Macron government if this instrument of state surveillance were made available to them! Survey agents report that these results are broadly similar to those obtained in Germany, the United Kingdom, and Italy.[77]

The "Stockholm Syndrome" on a Planetary Scale – Collective Diabolic Infestation?

The old 'carrot and stick' strategy is yielding results that would have been unimaginable just a few months ago. Suffice it to look at the panic caused by SARS-CoV-2 and people's sense of security at their governments' assurances that they will open the taps of public funding to secure individual incomes and keep companies solvent.

"What is happening, at this moment, is a strengthening of the State as a protective force for citizens," suggests *Isto é* in its above-cited article. Its title is expressive: "The New World Order: The State Is Once Again the Great Protective Force, and the Only One Capable of Creating a Robust System to Provide Security for the Citizen, Guaranteeing Health, Education, and Encouraging Scientific Research."[78]

Naivete goes so far as to apathetically accept a narrative of China's communist rulers presenting the regime as a model of success in controlling the pandemic that resulted from their own irresponsible, if not criminal attitudes. For example, no one reacted when the UN-issued *UN News* bulletin reported in its March 16 issue: "China shows COVID-19 Coronavirus can be 'stopped in its tracks.'" It quotes WHO's representative in that country: "This lesson in containment, therefore, is a lesson that other countries can learn from and adapt for their own circumstances."[79] Now, everyone knows that in China, the population is subjected to official social control policies through facial recognition and population rating programs, leading to prizes and punishments.

Only three months ago, the West's masses were inebriated with the values of emancipation, autonomy, and individualism. Today they accept the prospect of Chinese communist-style control of their lives with the passivity of lambs being led to the slaughterhouse reveals that they were victims of an ideological transshipment unprecedented in human history. Their natural reaction should be that of the philosopher Comte-Sponville in the interview above: "A stay at home order is the greatest restriction of freedom that I've experienced, and like everyone else, I'm in a hurry to get out of it. In the long run, there is not even a question of sacrificing freedom for the sake of health. I'd rather catch COVID-19 in a free country than be spared from it in a totalitarian state!"[80]

What radical ecologists, green parties, and the handlers of Greta Thunberg have achieved only partially (based on apocalyptic projections of consequences of the much-trumpeted and supposedly man-made global warming), the coronavirus panic plus protective nanny songs from governments "on the warpath" against the pandemic obtained after less than two months of widespread stay at home orders. As *Isto é* aptly put it, that "makes people experience a kind of house arrest not yet experienced in contemporary societies."[81]

That would be the Stockholm Syndrome on a global scale, whereby a kidnapped victim develops a relationship of complicity and a strong emotional bond with his or her kidnapper.[82] The proof is that, although they are ruining their economies through reckless stay at home orders, European leaders' approval ratings have surged: Kurz, Austria (+ 33%), Conte, Italy (+27%), Johnson, UK (+ 20%), Merkel, Germany (+11%), and Macron, France

$(+ 11\%)$.[83]

Faced with the dazzling, profound, and universal result obtained by this psychological manipulation of the masses, a Catholic observer must ask himself if it was not accompanied by a collective preternatural infestation. In 1959, Msgr. Léon Cristiani raised an analogous hypothesis concerning Chinese and Russian communism, in his book, *Evidence of Satan in the Modern World*. For the author, China manifested symptoms of diabolical possession. On the other hand, he thought Russia was the victim of preternatural infestation "only." However, he also believed that the West was under the influence of the Evil One.[84] Is the increase of this influence not one of the factors in the current passivity of world opinion, faced as it is with the possibility of a dictatorship? A dictatorship that is at first health-oriented, but which then becomes ecological and socialist, and finally, atheist?

A Forewarning Essay by Plinio Corrêa de Oliveira on Unperceived Ideological Transshipment

However dominant may be the role the preternatural factor plays in this passivity, it largely resulted from fear, leading the population to accept restrictions they would normally reject.

The best study on such mass manipulations – not from a preternatural, but a psychological and ideological perspective – is undoubtedly Plinio Corrêa de Oliveira's essay *Unperceived Ideological Transshipment and Dialogue, the Latest Communist Ploy to Conquer World Opinion*, published in the magazine *Catolicismo* (nos. 178 – 179, Oct. – Nov. 1965).[85]

In this work, the illustrious author describes the process to favorably predispose and transform people who resist *explicit* communist preaching into useful innocents. This is accomplished by acting *implicitly* upon their mentalities. That happens without patients realizing that they are suffering a psychological manipulation.

Two factors made the Western mindset especially vulnerable: *fear* and *sympathy* for
communism. Although seemingly contradictory, both acted simultaneously and in tandem,
initially predisposing the patient to an attitude
of resigned inertia in the face of the communist
advance. Later, that would turn into a favorable
expectation and reach its final stage with the
transformation of the victim into a convinced
follower.

For example, some Latin American
Catholics engaged in Catholic Action underwent a process of ideological transshipment.
They ended up adhering to Liberation Theology, and later became militants of radical left
groups advocating violent action.

The method – the Brazilian intellectual
explains – presupposes finding a point of strong
impressionability, for example, "a disaster like
famine or disease." At the same time, it is necessary to find a *point of apathy* that is symmetrical
to the point of impressionability.

In our coronavirus case, the reader

should take note of this paradox: Many of those who now uphold as a supreme value the lives of the elderly threatened by the virus are the same ones who until recently claimed the right of these same older people to euthanasia. Moreover, they advocate allowing women under shelter-in-place orders to abort at home, without restrictions, even if in the third trimester.

Another example of a point of apathy, Prof. Corrêa de Oliveira writes, would be "insensitivity to the fact that, if one should do everything possible against hunger and sickness – considered here as social evils – in no way should one try to do the impossible, the utopian, since this would only sooner or later aggravate the very same evils one desires to vanquish."

With prophetic words, the author warns that it is necessary to apply solutions "with redoubled concern to prevent the natural delay of the cure from being added to the censurable slowdown resulting from our negligence. But one must frequently give up the impatient desire for immediate results. This desire, in effect, exposes us to the risk of preferring, rather than authentic solutions, the violent panaceas extolled by demagogy and effective only in appearance."

All of this would seem to have been written yesterday about the coronavirus overreaction, rather than in 1965.

The Role of "Talismanic Words" and How to Exorcise Them

Prof. Corrêa de Oliveira continues. Having achieved this single issue fixation in the patient's mind, the process handlers must then choose some "talisman words." These must have a legitimate but artfully manipulated meaning that can evoke a constellation of emotions, sympathies, and phobias that the media can easily exploit and are likely to become strongly radicalized.

Here are some words currently employed and relentlessly repeated by the media: "shared responsibility," "global solidarity," "cooperative response," "global strategy," "inclusive protection," "universal basic income," "ecological conversion," "common home," and so on.

Gripped by the fascination of the "talismanic word," patients "quickly accept as supreme and ardently professed ideals, the successively more radical meanings that it assumes." The author illustrates his point with the word "dialogue." He deemed it responsible for all of the Catholic Church's surrenders in the face of the errors of the modern world. Yesterday, it was the dialogue with communism. Today, it is a dialogue with radical ecology, efforts to implement a secular world governance, and the radical left's "another world is possible."

Will the ongoing gigantic operation of social engineering and ideological transshipment succeed? If this process is based on the fear-sympathy syndrome, it is undeniable that the people's panic of SARS-CoV-2, plus the illusory comfort and sympathy that many of them draw from government promises of health and financial protection are likely to raise leftist strategists' hopes. Hopes of what? That they will be successful in leading millions to accept a "new world." It would be a supposedly less frantic and selfish new world, one that shows more solidarity, is closer to nature, but, above all, one that is more controlled by an ecological-socialist Big Brother.

However, that leftist victory is avoidable. Even as their plan is underway, one can pierce it like a balloon simply by "exorcizing" the talismanic words. This is done through analysis, explaining their meanings, and thus disturbing their victims' emotional enjoyment of the illegitimate meanings.

"[T]o 'exorcise' the talismanic word and incapacitate its magic effect," the Brazilian professor explains, "one must, first of all, discover the myth incubated in its many meanings and compare its most applauded and radiating meanings with its natural and common meaning to discover "the content of this word hidden in its mythical and radical meanings." Whoever makes explicit and unmasks the hidden myth "will provide the patients of unperceived ideological transshipment with sufficient means to open their eyes to the action worked on them, see where they are being led, and defend themselves against it."

One of the greatest difficulties faced by those wishing to carry out this enlightening and salvific work in the Catholic sphere is that Pope Francis and the Vatican are serving as fellow travelers for the promoters of the ongoing ideological transshipment.

The Role of the Religious Factor in the Process of Ideological Transshipment Toward the "New World"

In the current maneuver, there are two factors. First, the COVID-19 panic, and then, the "sympathy" factor, a romantic aspiration to leave the stress and individualism of the modern world and return to one more "respectful of nature," more "open" and "supportive," in which the luxury standards of industrialized "bourgeois" societies give way to the simplicity and frugality of the working class.

In fact, in a society as materialistic and hedonistic as ours, such change would be very transitory if driven only by panic, as Jacques Attali said in the above-cited text. However, popular resignation would be permanent and more profound if it considered the change as a spiritual improvement, not just something deemed inevitable to which one must resign oneself.

A minority of the population – the more "modern" and "advanced" parts of the middle and upper bourgeoisie that frequent "champagne socialist" circles could find such motivation in Eastern religions, yoga, vegetarianism, etc. But the sensible majority of the population needs to hear the voice of great religious leaders. In a mostly Catholic West, none can be better than the pope's. All the more so if it is packaged as an echo of the "Poor Man of Assisi."

Unfortunately, it is the game that Pope Francis is playing with his repeated calls in favor of integral ecology, a new globalization model, and "popular movements" as the leaven of future society.

Unfortunately, with his repeated calls for integral ecology, a new model of globalization, and "popular movements" as the leaven of future society, that is the game to which Pope Francis is lending himself.

Pope Francis Calls for "Ecological Conversion"

In fact, since the beginning of the SARS-CoV-2 epidemic, Pope Francis has missed no opportunity to support these three ideological currents.

On Sunday, March 22, the pontiff of *Laudato Si* gave a video interview to Spanish journalist Jordi Évole on his television program on the *La Sexta* channel. Asked if the coronavirus crisis was "a revenge of nature," Francis replied that nature never forgives and that it "is kicking us so we can take care of it."[86]

Two weeks later, the pope returned to the charge. In an interview with his biographer, Austen Ivereigh, published in *The Tablet*, the pontiff praised the governments that implemented "exemplary" stay at home measures. Asked if the economic devastation caused by the crisis was a chance for an ecological conversion, he repeated that "nature never forgives," and added: "We did not respond to the partial catastrophes. . . . I don't know if these are the revenge of nature, but they are certainly nature's response." Later on, he added: "You ask me about conversion. Every crisis contains both danger and opportunity: the opportunity to move out of the danger. Today I believe we have to slow down our rate of production and consumption (*Laudato Si*, no. 191) and to learn to understand and contemplate the natural world. We need to reconnect with our real surroundings. This is the opportunity for conversion."[87]

At the General Audience of April 22 – the UN's International Mother Earth Day – the Pope declared: "As the tragic coronavirus pandemic has taught us, we can overcome global challenges only by showing solidarity with one another and embracing the most vulnerable in our midst . . . Because of our selfishness we have failed in our responsibility to be guardians and stewards of the earth . . . We have polluted it, we have despoiled it, endangering our very lives. . . . We have sinned against the earth, against our neighbours, and ultimately against the Creator. . . . We need an ecological conversion that can find expression in concrete actions."

Pope Francis took the occasion to note that "various international and local movements have sprung up in order to appeal to our consciences" (notably the one led by figurehead by figurehead Greta Thunberg) and added, "It will be necessary for our children to take to the streets to teach us the obvious: we have no future if we destroy the very environment that sustains us."

Echoing the Synod of Bishops for the Pan-Amazon region, he added: "Today, as we celebrate World Earth Day, we are called to rediscover the sense of sacred respect for the earth, because it is not only our home but also God's home. This gives rise in us to the awareness that we are on a sacred earth!"

Earlier in the address, he repeated that the coronavirus is a response of nature:

> We have sinned against the earth, against our neighbors, and ultimately against the Creator, the benevolent Father who provides for everyone, and desires us to live in communion and flourish together. And how does the earth react? There is a Spanish saying that is very clear about this. It goes: 'God always forgives; we humans sometimes forgive, and sometimes not; the earth never forgives.' The

<blockquote>
earth does not forgive: if we have despoiled the earth, its response will be very ugly.[88]
</blockquote>

This idea of nature's revenge had already been put forward by Fr. Benedict Mayaki, who published an article in *Vatican News* titled "Coronavirus: Earth's Unlikely Ally." In it, the African Jesuit stated that "we have never treated our Common Home as badly as in the last two hundred years." Still, this epidemic "has an unintended benefit: the Earth is healing itself" since "changes in human behavior due to the COVID-19 virus pandemic are bringing unintended benefits to the planet."[89] Because of outraged protests from readers, the Vatican's media website withdrew the article an hour later.

However, Leonardo Boff was the one who first raised this hypothesis. In an article titled "Coronavirus: A Reprisal from Gaia, Mother Earth?" he stated:

<blockquote>
I estimate that current diseases such as dengue, chikungunya, zika virus, SARS, ebola, measles, the ongoing coronavirus and the widespread degradation in human relationships, marked by profound inequality/social injustice
</blockquote>

and the lack of minimal solidarity, are a reprisal from Gaia for the offenses that we continuously inflict on her. I would not say, like J. Lovelock, that it is 'the revenge of Gaia,' since she as Great Mother does not take revenge but gives us severe signs that she is sick (typhoons, melting polar ice caps, droughts, and floods, etc.) and, at the limit, she sends us a reprisal like the referred-to diseases because we do not learn the lesson.[90]

The Vatican Aligns Itself With the Promoters of Global Governance

The Pontifical Academy of Sciences and the Pontifical Academy of Social Sciences, both headed by Bishop Marcelo Sánchez Sorondo, an Argentine prelate very close to Pope Francis, issued a significant statement on the Vatican's support for plans to globalize the response to the crisis.

The March 20 statement calls on people to fully support the propaganda of international organizations such as WHO and UNICEF, so that "their scientific evidence-based information can rise above the cacophony of unproven assumptions spreading all over the world." It goes on to express concern about the "selfishness and shortsightedness of uncoordinated national responses."

In the section titled "**Shaping global interdependencies and help across and within nations**," the statement finds that "globalism has made the world unprecedentedly interdependent – and thus vulnerable . . . during crises." But, it adds, "seeking protection through isolationism would be misguided and counter-productive," whereas "A trend worth backing would be a strong demand for greater global cooperation," and the support for international organizations. "Global problems such as pandemics or the less visible crises of global climate change and biodiversity loss demand global cooperative responses," says the document, insisting that " global crises demand collective action" and that "The prevention and containment of pandemics is a *global public good* (*Laudato Si*) and protecting it requires increased global coordination."

It concludes by asserting that, "At a time when rule-based multilateralism is declining, the COVID-19 crisis should encourage efforts to bring about a new – in the sense of different – globalization model aimed at inclusive protection of all." This, in a "more responsible, more sharing, more equalitarian, more caring and fairer society. . . if we are to survive."[91]

Bill Gates, Antônio Guterres, and Gordon Brown, great promoters of a new world order under the UN aegis, would have no difficulty subscribing to this declaration by the two Vatican Academies, which includes no mention of God.

Along the same lines is a statement of which the *Osservatore Romano* published a summary. Issued by the Academy of Catholic Leaders, an entity born in Chile and present in several countries in Latin America, it was signed by 170 individuals, including Italian philosopher Rocco Butiglione and the Uruguayan Guzmán Carriquiry, vice president emeritus of the Pontifical Commission for Latin America.[92] In it, the self-described Catholic leaders affirm, in a Bolivarian tone that would have pleased Hugo Chavez, that "if problems are common, it is necessary to think about common solutions and initiatives. Either we die alone as nations, or we advance as all nations together as members of the same Great Fatherland: Latin America.

He continues: "If we choose the path of exacerbated nationalism, our countries are bound to plunge into chaos, populism, and authoritarianism. But if we choose the path of the Great Fatherland precisely as most of our countries celebrate the Bicentennial of their processes of independence, it will be an opportunity to re-found a new social pact based on solidarity and fraternity." They repeat the leftist mantra of universal basic income, even if for a limited time: "We support the need for a temporary basic income that guarantees a life above the poverty line." And, obviously enough, they imperatively conclude that "all governments in Latin America must make a formal and rigorous commitment to the instructions issued by the Pan American Health Organization during the pandemic."[93]

Pope Francis to the Extreme Left: "I'm Available to Lend a Hand"

Pope Francis's support for the postulates of the radical left, of which he has become the undisputed international leader,[94] was evident in letters he wrote to Luca Casarini and, on Easter Sunday, to Popular Movements.

Casarini was the leader of the "No-Global" protests that destroyed Genoa during the G8 meeting of July 2001. He is currently the regional secretary for the *Sinistra Italiana* (Italian Left) party and responsible for the organization *Mediterranea – Saving Humans,* which advocates admitting illegal immigrants into Italy. However, because of the pandemic, the Union's borders are closed even for Europeans from the Schengen Area. On April 11, it was reported that Pope Francis sent Casarini a handwritten note in which he thanks "Dear Brother" for "his testimony, which has done me so much good." And he concludes: "I want to tell you that I'm always available to lend a hand. Count on me."[95]

Even more eloquent was his letter addressed on Easter Sunday to "dear friends" of "popular movements and organizations" around the world. In it, Pope Francis points out that "This may be the time to consider a universal basic income[96] which would acknowledge and dignify the noble, essential tasks you carry out."

The pope added, "If the fight against the coronavirus is a war, you are a true invisible army that fights in the most dangerous trenches." "An army with no other weapon than solidarity, hope, and the sense of community that grows green these days when no one is saved alone."

In a vague nod to the ecological and self-managing utopias of popular movements (such as Brazil's MST or Argentina's *cartoneros*), the pope expresses his hope that "governments understand that technocratic paradigms (whether State- or market-centric) are not enough to address this crisis or the other major problems of humanity." Because, he continues, "now more than ever, it is persons, communities, peoples who must be at the center, united to heal, care, share." He goes on to say that popular movements "have an authoritative voice to testify" that change is possible, and asks them to "continue the struggle."[97]

For its part, the Dicastery for Promoting Integral Human Development presided over by Peter Cardinal Turkson – in collaboration with two other agencies of the Holy See and notably the two Academies headed by Bishop Sánchez Sorondo – created five working groups to prepare for the aftermath of COVID-19. The second group "has the task of the night watch, like the sentry, to perceive the dawn," the Ghanaian cardinal says. "To do this, it is necessary to connect the best minds in the areas of ecology, economy, health, and public security;" we "need prophecy, and creativity. We need to go above and beyond."

Crises may follow one after the other, "in a cycle in which we will be forced to learn slowly and painfully [to] take care of our common home, as Pope Francis so prophetically teaches in the Encyclical *Laudato Si*. There is a need for courage, for prophecy." Because "inhabiting the Earth as a common home requires much more. It requires solidarity in accessing the goods of creation as a 'common good,' and solidarity in applying the fruits of research and technology to make our 'Home' healthier and more livable for all," concluded Cardinal Turkson, with a language close to that of green parties and the radical left.[98]

If This Worldwide Maneuver Succeeds, God's Punishment Is Inevitable – but Our Lady Will Triumph!

The ideological transshipment that Plinio Corrêa de Oliveira denounced in 1965 was highly successful within the Catholic Church. The manipulation of the talismanic word "dialogue" led many sectors of the clergy and part of the laity to sympathize with socialism and communism. What were the results? Ill-fated liberation theology and the heterodox forms of ecumenism and interreligious dialogue informing the Declaration of Abu Dhabi, among others. But the maneuver failed on the political plane, because the Europeans did not allow themselves to be duped by a "Eurocommunism" with a human face, nor did Latin Americans fall for "Christian socialism." The internal crisis behind the Iron Curtain and the arms race led to the collapse of the USSR and the recycling of communism into cultural neo-Marxism.

This ideological transshipment maneuver might be more successful in the current situation, characterized by panic. If that happens, even temporarily, an ecological and socialist "new world order" (either centralized or self-managing) could be imposed on humanity with the Vatican's blessings.

In that case, humanity would undoubtedly deserve a great punishment whose preamble would have been the current pandemic. Some high-ranking prelates have come out strongly against the opinion that the coronavirus crisis is the hand of Divine Providence punishing the world for today's immense sins – procured abortion, same-sex "marriage," and civil unions, blasphemies of all kinds. These ecclesiastics claim that God could not indiscriminately punish both the just and sinners as COVID-19 does.

Plinio Corrêa de Oliveira answers this objection in a footnote of his work, *Unperceived Ideological Transshipment and Dialogue.* All the reader needs to do is to replace the term "thermonuclear catastrophe" with "pandemic," "economic ruin," or "ecological and socialist new world order" and he will have an updated version of this warning by the Brazilian Catholic leader.

After affirming that accepting the establishment of communism around the world to save peace (accepting the "new world order" to prevent COVID-19, we would say) would be a serious violation of the Law of God, the illustrious author writes:

> This supreme sin, precisely on being committed by nations and not only by individuals, is subject to Divine Justice in a very special way.
>
> Indeed, while the sins of individuals can be punished in this world or the next, it is not that way with the sins of nations. As St. Augustine says, since nations cannot be rewarded or punished in the next life, they are rewarded for their good actions and punished for their bad actions here on earth.
>
> Thus, in terms of justice, to a supreme sin of countries corresponds a supreme punishment in this world. And this could well be a thermonuclear catastrophe.
>
> There is more danger of such a catastrophe in apostasy than fidelity.

> This affirmation will be even better
> proven if we consider not only the
> punishment but also the reward. Na-
> tions faithful to the Law of God should
> receive just recompense on this earth.
> Nothing then is more suitable to at-
> tract the protection and favor of God
> to a nation, even regarding the goods
> of this life, than heroic fidelity in the
> face of a thermo-nuclear danger. This
> fidelity is the means par excellence to
> drive this danger away.

To steer clear of a well-deserved punishment from Divine Justice through new and even more lethal waves of SARS-CoV-2, let us avoid being dominated by panic and the greatest operation of unperceived ideological transshipment in history, even though this maneuver enjoys Vatican support.

Indeed, we must stand fast and refuse the "new world order" that the sirens of ecologism, globalism, and neo-socialism are offering us. We will thus remain faithful to the Law of God and the Divine Master's counsel: "Seek ye therefore first the kingdom of God, and his justice, and all these things shall be added unto you" (Matt. 6:33).

It is this fidelity that will help advance the fulfillment of the great promise that Our Lady of Fatima made to the world at the Cova da Iria:

"Finally, My Immaculate Heart will triumph!"

ENDNOTES

1 Alberto Rossi, "Coronavirus, l'allarme delle esperti: "Un terzo del mondo sarà contagiato. Milioni i morti," *Teleclubitalia.it*, Feb. 17, 2020, https://www.teleclubitalia.it/185547/coronavirus-lallarme-delle-esperti-un-terzo-del-mondo-sara-contagiato-milioni-i-morti/.

2 Francesco Sisci, "Scenario Coronavirus/ L'Italia non è la Cina, ma deve cambiare passo: con la Nato," Mar. 9, 2020, https://www.ilsussidiario.net/news/scenario-coronavirus-litalia-non-e-la-cina-ma-deve-cambiare-passo-con-la-nato/1994403/.

3 Imperial College COVID-19 Response Team, "Report 9: Impact of Non-Pharmaceutical Interventions (NPIs) to Reduce COVID-19 Mortality and Healthcare Demand," *Imperial.ac.uk*, 3, Mar. 16, 2020, https://www.imperial.ac.uk/media/imperial-college/medicine/sph/ide/gida-fellowships/Imperial-College-COVID19-NPI-modelling-16-03-2020.pdf.

4 See Douglas Jordan, Terrence Tumpey, and Barbara Jester, "The Deadliest Flu: The Complete Story of the Discovery and Reconstruction of the 1918 Pandemic Virus," *CDC.gov*, accessed Apr. 27, 2020, https://www.cdc.gov/flu/pandemic-resources/reconstruction-1918-virus.html.

5 Neil Ferguson, *Twitter*, accessed Apr. 26, 2020, https://twitter.com/neil_ferguson/status/1241835454707699713.

6 See Benny Peiser and Andrew Montford, "Coronavirus Lessons From the Asteroid That Didn't Hit Earth," *The Wall Street Journal*, Apr. 1, 2020, https://www.wsj.com/articles/coronavirus-lessons-from-the-asteroid-that-didnt-hit-earth-11585780465.

7 See Matt Stieb, "Oxford Model: Coronavirus May Have Already Infected Half of U.K. Population," *New York Intelligencer*, Mar. 24, 2020, https://nymag.com/intelligencer/2020/03/oxford-study-coronavirus-may-have-infected-half-of-u-k.html.

8 Thomas Wider, "Coronavirus : une étude dans le principal foyer de l'épidémie en Allemagne revoit le taux de mortalité à la baisse," *Le Monde*, Apr. 10, 2020, https://www.lemonde.fr/planete/article/2020/04/10/coronavirus-une-etude-allemande-revoit-a-la-baisse-le-taux-de-mortalite_6036206_3244.html.

9 See Anna Otte, Anthony C. Marriott, Carola Dreier, et al. "Evolution of 2009 H1N1 Influenza Viruses During the Pandemic Correlates With

Increased Viral Pathogenicity and Transmissibility in the Ferret Model," *Nature*, Jun. 24, 2016, https://www.nature.com/articles/srep28583.

10 "Coronavirus, il quadro clinico dei deceduti in Italia," *Tg24.Sky.it*, Mar. 6, 2020, https://tg24.sky.it/salute-e-benessere/2020/03/06/coronavirus-deceduti-italia.html.

11 Chiara Lanari, "Coronavirus, drammatiche previsioni Istat: rischio shock economico," *Investireoggi*, Apr. 8, 2020, https://www.investireoggi.it/economia/coronavirus-drammatiche-previsioni-istat-rischio-shock-economico/.

12 Bruno Perini, "COVID-19: depressione economica, c'è chi sente già l'odore," *SenzaFiltro*, Apr. 8, 2020, https://www.informazionesenzafiltro.it/covid-19-depressione-economica-ce-chi-sente-gia-lodore/.

13 Gustavo Boni, "La crisi del coronavirus: che ne sarà di noi?" *Osservatorioglobalizzazione.it*, Apr. 6, 2020, http://osservatorioglobalizzazione.it/dossier/coronavirus-sfide-e-scenari/la-crisi-del-coronavirus-che-ne-sara-di-noi/.

14 Perini, "Depressione economica," https://www.informazionesenzafiltro.it/covid-19-depressione-economica-ce-chi-sente-gia-lodore/.

15 Paolo Baroni, "Coronavirus "choc epocale": in Italia a rischio 1 milione di imprese," *La Stampa*, Apr. 7, 2020, https://www.lastampa.it/economia/lavoro/2020/04/07/news/coronavirus-choc-epocale-in-italia-a-rischio-1-milione-di-imprese-1.38689190.

16 Lanari, "Rischio shock economico," https://www.investireoggi.it/economia/coronavirus-drammatiche-previsioni-istat-rischio-shock-economico/.

17 Marc Vignaud, "Coronavirus : l'activité chute de 36 % en France," *Le Point*, Apr. 9, 2020, https://www.lepoint.fr/economie/coronavirus-l-activite-chute-de-36-en-france-09-04-2020-2370770_28.php#.

18 Nicolas Baverez, "'Le déconfinement, une urgence nationale,'" *Le Figaro*, Apr. 19, 2020, https://www.lefigaro.fr/vox/societe/nicolas-baverez-le-deconfinement-une-urgence-nationale-20200419.

19 Océane Herrero, "9,6 millions de salariés du privé sont au chômage partiel, annonce Muriel Pénicaud," *Le Figaro*, Apr. 20, 2020, https://www.lefigaro.fr/flash-eco/9-6-millions-de-salaries-du-prive-sont-au-chomage-partiel-annonce-muriel-penicaud-20200420.

20 Audrey Tonnelier, "Les conséquences, par secteur économique,

du confinement des Français," *Le Monde*, Apr. 7, 2020, https://www.le-monde.fr/politique/article/2020/04/07/les-consequences-par-secteur-economique-du-confinement-des-francais_6035832_823448.html.

21 "Coronavirus : l'impact économique de l'épidémie sera "considérable», prévient Philippe," *Le Parisien*, Apr. 8, 2020, http://www.leparisien.fr/economie/coronavirus-l-impact-economique-de-l-epidemie-sera-considerable-previent-philippe-08-04-2020-8296404.php.

22 "Le coronavirus provoque 'les pires conséquences économiques' depuis 1929, prévient le FMI," *L'Obs*, Apr. 9, 2020, https://www.nouvelobs.com/coronavirus-de-wuhan/20200409.OBS27303/le-coronavirus-provoque-les-pires-consequences-economiques-depuis-1929-previent-le-fmi.html

23 Julien Bouissou, "Coronavirus : le FMI prédit une récession mondiale historique, avec un recul de la croissance estimé à 3% en 2020," *Le Monde*, Apr. 14, 2020, https://www.lemonde.fr/economie/article/2020/04/14/coronavirus-le-fmi-predit-une-recession-mondiale-historique-avec-un-recul-de-la-croissance-estime-a-3-en-2020_6036559_3234.html

24 "COVID-19 and the world of work."Second edition. https://www.ilo.org/wcmsp5/groups/public/@dgreports/@dcomm/documents/briefing-note/wcms_740877.pdf.

25   https://www.ilo.org/global/about-the-iglo/newsroom/news/WCMS_740893/lang – en/index.htm

26 Anne Cheyvialle, "Le Covid-19 provoque une envolée du chômage dans le monde," *Le Monde*, Apr. 7, 2020, https://www.lefigaro.fr/social/coronavirus-1-25-milliard-de-travailleurs-courent-un-risque-de-licenciement-ou-de-reduction-de-salaire-selon-l-oit-20200407.

27 Pierre-Yves Dugua, "Le Covid-19 met à terre l'économie américaine," *Le Figaro*, Apr. 16, 2020, https://www.lefigaro.fr/conjoncture/le-covid-19-met-a-terre-l-economie-americaine-20200416.

28 Sébastian Seibt, "Coronavirus: 500 millions de personnes menacées par la pauvreté, 'aucun équivalent historique,'" *France24.com*, Apr. 9, 2020, https://www.france24.com/fr/20200409-coronavirus-500-millions-de-personnes-menac%C3%A9es-par-la-pauvret%C3%A9-aucun-%C3%A9quivalent-historique.

29 Bouissou, "le FMI prédit une récession," https://www.lemonde.fr/economie/article/2020/04/14/coronavirus-le-fmi-predit-une-reces-

sion-mondiale-historique-avec-un-recul-de-la-croissance-estime-a-3-en-2020_6036559_3234.html.

30 Organisation for Economic Co-operation and Development and World Health Organization, "Poverty and Health," [DAC Guidelines and Reference Series], *WHO.int*, 14, accessed Apr. 27, 2020, https://www.who.int/tobacco/research/economics/publications/oecd_dac_pov_health.pdf.

31 "Global Hunger Could Double Due to COVID-19 Blow: U.N.," *Reuters*, Apr. 21, 2020, https://www.reuters.com/article/us-health-corona-virus-un-food/global-hunger-could-double-due-to-covid-19-blow-u-n-idUSKBN22313U.

32 Fiona Harvey, "Coronavirus Pandemic 'Will Cause Famine of Biblical Proportions,'" *The Guardian*, Apr. 21, 2020, https://www.theguardian.com/global-development/2020/apr/21/coronavirus-pandemic-will-cause-famine-of-biblical-proportions.

33 See, for example, Peter-Philipp Schmitt, „Wir haben neue Symptome entdeckt" *Frankfurter Allgemeine*, Mar. 6, 2020, https://www.faz.net/aktuell/gesellschaft/gesundheit/coronavirus/neue-coro-na-symptome-entdeckt-virologe-hendrik-streeck-zum-virus-16681450.html and Hugo Martin, "Para un prestigioso científico argentino, 'el coronavirus no merece que el planeta esté en un estado de parate total,'" *Infobae*, Mar. 28, 2020, https://www.infobae.com/coronavirus/2020/03/28/para-un-prestigioso-cientifico-argentino-el-coronavirus-no-merece-que-el-planeta-este-en-un-estado-de-parate-total/.

34 See Audrey Wison, "The Countries That Are Succeeding at Flattening the Curve," *Foreign Policy*, Apr. 2, 2020, https://foreignpolicy.com/2020/04/02/countries-succeeding-flattening-curve-coronavirus-testing-quarantine/.

35 Stefano Magni, "Lockdown: gli italiani sono i più reclusi del mondo," *La Nuova Bussola Quotidiana*, Apr. 15, 2020, https://lanuovabq.it/it/lockdown-gli-italiani-sono-i-piu-reclusi-del-mondo.

36 The Editorial Board, "Rethinking the Coronavirus Shutdown," *The Wall Street Journal*, Mar. 19, 2020, https://www.wsj.com/articles/rethinking-the-coronavirus-shutdown-11584659154.

37 https://istoe.com.br/a-nova-ordem-mundial/

38 World Health Organization, "Guiding Principles for Immunization Activities During the COVID-19 Pandemic, *WHO.int*, Mar. 26,

2020, https://apps.who.int/iris/bitstream/handle/10665/331590/WHO-2019-nCoV-immunization_services-2020.1-eng.pdf. (Emphasis in the original.)

39 Javier Sampedro, "El dilema del diablo," *El País*, Apr. 10, 2020, https://elpais.com/ciencia/2020-04-10/el-dilema-del-diablo.html

40 *Ibid.*

41 Julio Loredo, "Le grandi lezioni di un piccolo essere," *Associazione Tradizione Famiglia Proprietà*, accessed Apr. 28, 2020, http://atfp.it/varie/1722-le-grandi-lezioni-di-un-piccolo-essere.

42 John Gray, "Why This Crisis Is a Turning Point in History," *New-Statesman*, Apr. 1, 2020, https://www.newstatesman.com/international/2020/04/why-crisis-turning-point-history.

43 Paola Estrada, "Guerra ao imperialismo e ao coronavírus na América Latina," *MST*, Apr. 10, 2020, https://mst.org.br/2020/04/10/guerra-ao-imperialismo-e-ao-coronavirus-na-america-latina/.

44 François Gemenne and Anneliese Depoux, "'De la crise du coronavirus, on peut tirer des leçons pour lutter contre le changement climatique,'" *Le Monde*, Mar. 18, 2020, https://www.lemonde.fr/idees/article/2020/03/18/de-la-crise-du-coronavirus-on-peut-tirer-des-lecons-pour-lutter-contre-le-changement-climatique_6033464_3232.html; see also Beth Gardiner, "Coronavirus Holds Key Lessons on How to Fight Climate Change," *e360.Yale.edu*, Mar. 23, 2020, https://e360.yale.edu/features/coronavirus-holds-key-lessons-on-how-to-fight-climate-change.

45 Gemenne and Depoux, "'De la crise du coronavirus,'" https://www.lemonde.fr/idees/article/2020/03/18/de-la-crise-du-coronavirus-on-peut-tirer-des-lecons-pour-lutter-contre-le-changement-climatique_6033464_3232.html

46 Blanca Ruibal, Luis Rico García-Amado, Mario Rodríguez, Asunción Ruiz, and Juan Carlos del Olmo, "Una reconstrucción económica por la salud del planeta y de las personas," *El País*, Apr. 19, 2020, https://elpais.com/sociedad/2020-04-19/una-reconstruccion-economica-por-la-salud-del-planeta-y-de-las-personas.html.

47 Manuel Planelles, "Nace una gran alianza europea para defender una salida verde a la crisis económica del coronavirus," *El País*, Apr. 14, 2020, https://elpais.com/sociedad/2020-04-14/nace-una-gran-alianza-europea-para-defender-una-salida-verde-a-la-crisis-economi-

ca-del-corononavirus.html.

48 Bill Gates, "Una estrategia mundial contra la Covid-19," *El País*, Apr. 11, 2020, https://elpais.com/elpais/2020/04/11/opinion/1586600730_628755.html.

49 Jeanne Smits, "Coronavirus: le rapport de l'ONU qui annonce la globalisation des solutions en vue d'une société 'plus égalitaire et plus inclusive,'" *Reinformation.TV*, Apr. 9, 2020, https://reinformation.tv/coronavirus-rapport-onu-globalisation-smits-90558-2/; see also "Shared Responsibility, Global Solidarity:Responding to the socio-economic impacts of COVID-19," *UNSDG.UN.org*, Mar. 2020, https://unsdg.un.org/sites/default/files/2020-03/SG-Report-Socio-Economic-Impact-of-Covid19.pdf.

50 Larry Elliott, "Gordon Brown Calls for Global Government to Tackle Coronavirus," *The Guardian*, Mar. 26, 2020, https://www.theguardian.com/politics/2020/mar/26/gordon-brown-calls-for-global-government-to-tackle-coronavirus.

51 Rafa de Miguel, "Gordon Brown: "No bastan las buenas palabras. Necesitamos un G20 con poderes ejecutivos que pase a la acción," *El País*, Apr. 18, 2020, https://elpais.com/ideas/2020-04-18/no-bastan-las-buenas-palabras-necesitamos-un-g20-con-poderes-ejecutivos-que-pase-a-la-accion.html.

52 "Declaração – III Reunião do Grupo de Puebla – Progressismo é Humanidade," *Grupo de Puebla*, Apr. 10, 2020, https://pt.org.br/wp-content/uploads/2020/04/declaracion-final-encuentro-virtual-grupo-de-puebla.pdf.

53 Naomi Klein, "Coronavirus Capitalism – And How to Beat It," *The Intercept*, Mar. 16, 2020, https://theintercept.com/2020/03/16/coronavirus-capitalism/.

54 Nicola Mirenzi, "Il Virus Dell'Avvenire. Slavoj Zizek e il Bisogno di 'un Nuovo Comunismo,'" *HuffingtonPost.it*, Apr. 8, 2020, https://www.huffingtonpost.it/entry/il-virus-dellavvenire_it_5e8d7c80c5b6e1a2e0fc234d

55 Isabel Acosta and Carmen Obregón, "Iglesias quiso aprovechar la alarma para nacionalizar eléctricas y hospitales," *El Economista*, Mar. 16, 2020, 6, https://s03.s3c.es/pdf/f/a/fa5c6ca439283c3e816c-577d39ad2f4a_superlunes.pdf.

56 Michael Severance, "Reddito universale? Non bastano le buone

intenzioni," *La Nuova Bussola Quotidiana*, Apr. 22, 2020, https://lanuovabq.it/it/reddito-universale-non-bastano-le-buone-intenzioni.

57 "Responder a la emergencia y evitar la dependencia," *Cope*, Apr. 21, 2020, https://www.cope.es/actualidad/linea-editorial/noticias/responder-emergencia-evitar-dependencia-20200421_690206.

58 See Mark Gilbert, "Helicopter Money," *Bloomberg.com*, Aug. 30, 2019, https://www.bloomberg.com/quicktake/helicopter-money.

59 "Benoît Hamon: 'Notre société s'est lourdement trompée en préférant les biens aux liens,'" *Le Monde*, Apr. 16, 2020, https://www.lemonde.fr/idees/article/2020/04/16/benoit-hamon-notre-societe-s-est-lourdement-trompee-en-preferant-les-biens-aux-liens_6036725_3232.html.

60 "Why More Than 500 Political Figures and Academics Globally Have Called for Universal Basic Income in the Fight Against Coronavirus," *Independent*, Mar. 18, 2020, https://www.independent.co.uk/voices/letters/coronavirus-universal-basic-income-ubi-poverty-economy-business-migrants-a9408846.html.

61 Maurizio Milano, "L'errore del socialismo di guerra per uscire dall'epidemia," La Nuova Bussola Quotidiana, Apr. 17, 2020, https://lanuovabq.it/it/lerrore-del-socialismo-di-guerra-per-uscire-dallepidemia

62 Beppe Grillo, "Reddito Universale: è arrivato il momento," *beppegrillo.it*, Mar. 30, 2020, https://www.beppegrillo.it/reddito-universale-e-arrivato-il-momento/.

63 Guillaume Larrivé, " 'Contre la guerre civile, pour l'union nationale.' La Tribune de Guillaume Larrivé, *l'Opinion*, Apr. 11, 2020, https://www.lopinion.fr/edition/politique/contre-guerre-civile-l-union-nationale-tribune-guillaume-larrive-215915. (Our emphasis.)

64 "Les services de renseignement s'inquiètent d'une radicalisation de la contestation sociale après le confinement," *Atlantico*, Apr. 12, 2020, https://www.atlantico.fr/pepite/3588764/les-services-de-renseignement-s-inquietent-d-une-radicalisation-de-la-contestation-sociale-apres-le-confinement.

65 Jean Chichizola, "Les violences contre la police se multiplient dans les cités," *Le Figaro*, Apr. 19, 2020, https://www.lefigaro.fr/actualite-france/les-violences-contre-la-police-se-multiplient-dans-les-cites-20200419.

66 Roberto de Mattei, "New Scenarios in the Coronavirus Era," *Lepanto Foundation*, Mar. 14, 2020, https://www.patreon.com/posts/new-sce-

narios-in-34876378, 9:01 – 9:35.

67 Jacques Attali, "Changer, par Précaution," *Attali.com*, May 3, 2019, http://www.attali.com/societe/changer-par-precaution/. (Our emphasis.)

68 Rachel Grumman Bender, *Yahoo!Life*, Feb. 6, 2020, https://www.yahoo.com/lifestyle/the-flu-has-killed-10000-americans-as-the-world-worries-over-coronavirus-221101770.html.

69 Simon Brunfaut, "André Comte-Sponville: 'J'aime mieux attraper le Covid-19 dans un pays libre qu'y échapper dans un État totalitaire,'" *L'Echo*, Apr. 27, 2020, https://www.lecho.be/dossiers/coronavirus/andre-comte-sponville-j-aime-mieux-attraper-le-covid-19-dans-un-pays-libre-qu-y-echapper-dans-un-etat-totalitaire/10221597.html

70 "Coronavirus: Five-year-old Among Latest UK Victims," *BBC*, Apr. 4, 2020, https://www.bbc.com/news/uk-52165443.

71 "Renaud Girard: 'Le confinement, remède pire que le mal?'" *Le Figaro*, Apr. 6, 2020, https://www.lefigaro.fr/vox/monde/renaud-girard-le-confinement-remede-pire-que-le-mal-20200406

72 "Coronavirus, la Diocesi di Roma chiude le chiese," *La Stampa*, Mar. 12, 2020, https://www.lastampa.it/cronaca/2020/03/12/news/coronavirus-la-diocesi-di-roma-chiude-le-chiese-1.38585371.

73 "Épidémie du coronavirus ou épidémie de peur?" *Group Siloé/ Source et Lumière de Siloé*, Mar. 6, 2020, http://siloe37.over-blog.com/2020/03/epidemie-du-coronavirus-ou-epidemie-de-peur.html.

74 François-Xavier Bourmaud, "Coronavirus: 96% des Français approuvent les mesures de confinement annoncées par Macron," *Le Figaro*, Mar. 19, 2020, https://www.lefigaro.fr/politique/coronavirus-96-des-francais-approuvent-les-mesures-de-confinement-annoncees-par-macron-20200319.

75 "Un 59% de los españoles apoya el confinamiento más estricto," *El País*, Apr. 18, 2020, https://elpais.com/espana/2020-04-18/los-ciudadanos-priman-la-salud-sobre-la-economia-y-apoyan-el-rescate-social.html.

76 Cyrille Louis, "Dans les pays riches, la santé reste la priorité," *Le Figaro*, Apr. 16, 2020, https://www.lefigaro.fr/international/dans-les-pays-riches-la-sante-reste-la-priorite-20200416.

77 Johannes Abeler, Sam Altmann, Luke Milsom, Séverine Toussaert,

Hannah Zillessen, "Acceptabilité d'une application téléphone pour tracer les contactsporteurs du Covid-19," *OSF*, Apr. 6, 2020, https://osf.io/24uan/

78 Vicente Vilardaga e Eudes Lima, "A nova ordem mundial," *Isto é*, Apr. 17, 2020, https://istoe.com.br/a-nova-ordem-mundial/.

79 "China Shows COVID-19 Coronavirus Can Be 'Stopped in its Tracks,'" UN.org, Mar. 16, 2020, https://news.un.org/en/story/2020/03/1059502.

80 Brunfaut, "André Comte-Sponville: 'J'aime mieux, *L'Echo*, https://www.lecho.be/dossiers/coronavirus/andre-comte-sponville-j-aime-mieux-attraper-le-covid-19-dans-un-pays-libre-qu-y-echapper-dans-un-etat-totalitaire/10221597.html.

81 Vilardaga e Lima, "A nova ordem mundial," *Isto é*, https://istoe.com.br/a-nova-ordem-mundial/.

82 See, Wikipedia contributors, "Stockholm syndrome," *Wikipedia, The Free Encyclopedia*, https://en.wikipedia.org/w/index.php?title=Stockholm_syndrome&oldid=953266399 (accessed

April 27, 2020.

83 Steven Erlanger, "Coronavirus Has Lifted Leaders Everywhere. Don't Expect That to Last," *The New York Times*, Apr. 15, 2020, https://www.nytimes.com/2020/04/15/world/europe/coronavirus-presidents.html.

84 Leon Cristiani, *Evidence of Satan in the Modern World*, https://www.ewtn.com/catholicism/library/evidence-of-satan-in-the-modern-world-6071, especially chapter 9.

85 Plinio Corrêa de Oliveira, *Unperceived Ideological Transshipment and Dialogue*, TFP.org, https://www.tfp.org/unperceived-ideological-transshipment-and-dialogue/.

86 Mateo González Alonso, "El papa Francisco a Évole sobre el coronavirus: 'Dios perdona siempre, nosotros a veces y la naturaleza nunca,'" *VidaNuevaDigital.com*, Mar. 23, 2020, https://www.vidanuevadigital.com/2020/03/23/el-papa-francisco-a-evole-sobre-el-coronavirus-dios-perdona-siempre-nosotros-a-veces-y-la-naturaleza-nunca/.

87 Austen Ivereigh, "Pope Francis Says Pandemic Can Be a 'Place of Conversion,'" *The Tablet*, Apr. 8, 2020, https://www.thetablet.co.uk/features/2/17845/pope-francis-says-pandemic-can-be-a-place-of-

conversion-

88 Pope Francis, "General Audience," *Vatican.va*, 8:35 – 18:00, Apr. 22, 2020, http://www.vatican.va/content/francesco/fr/audiences/2020/documents/papa-francesco_20200422_udienza-generale.html

89 Franca Giansoldati, "Coronavirus, le tesi choc di un gesuita che imbarazza il Vaticano: il Covid-19 fa bene all'ambiente," *Il Messaggero*, Apr. 1, 2020, https://www.ilmessaggero.it/vaticano/coronavirus_vaticano_fa_bene_all_ambiente_gesuita_vatican_news-5145977.html.

90 Leonardo Boff, "Coronavirus: uma represália de Gaia,da Mãe Terra?" *Leonardoboff.org*, Mar. 11, 2020, https://leonardoboff.org/2020/03/11/coronavirus-uma-represalia-de-gaiada-mae-terra/.

91 The Pontifical Academy of Sciences, "Responding to the Pandemic, Lessons for Future Actions and Changing Priorities, *PAS.va*, Mar. 20, 2020, http://www.pas.va/content/accademia/en/events/2020/coronavirus.html.

92 "Manifesto dei leader cattolici dell'America Latina," *VaticanNews.va*, Apr. 15, 2020, https://www.vaticannews.va/it/vaticano/news/2020-04/manifesto-leader-cattolici-america-latina-osservatore-romano.html.

93 "Manifiesto de Católicos Latinoamericanos con Responsabilidades Políticas: Un Compromiso y un Llamado a la Acción," http://liderescatolicos.net/manifiesto/Manifiesto_politico_latinoamericanos_Completo.pdf.

94 See Francis X. Rocca, "How Pope Francis Became the Leader of the Global Left" *The Wall Street Journal*, Dec. 22, 2016, https://www.wsj.com/articles/how-pope-francis-became-the-leader-of-the-global-left-1482431940.

95 https://www.ilgiornale.it/news/cronache/papa-ong-grazie-che-fate-contate-su-me-1852920.html

96 Spanish Vice President Pablo Iglesias criticized the reluctance of his country's bishops to support permanent universal basic income, saying, "I stick to what the pope said, who has again demonstrated enormous social sensitivity by presenting the need for everyone to have a vital minimum income. And until further notice, the pope is the head of the Catholic Church." "Pablo Iglesias defiende la renta mínima permanente y les dice a los obispos españoles que "hasta nueva orden» su jefe es el Papa," *InfoCatólica*, Apr. 23, 2020, http://www.

infocatolica.com/?t=noticia&cod=37502.

97 "Pope Francis sends letter in support of social movements," Radio Bayamo, Apr. 13, 2020, http://www.radiobayamo.icrt.cu/en/2020/04/13/pope-francis-sends-letter-in-support-of-social-movements/; see also, Washington Uranga, "La carta del papa Francisco a los movimientos populares del mundo," *Página 12*, Apr. 12, 2020, https://www.pagina12.com.ar/259242-la-carta-del-papa-francisco-a-los-movimientos-populares-del-.

98 Massimiliano Menichetti, "We Must Think of the Aftermath of COVID-19 so We Are Not Unprepared," Vatican News, Apr. 15, 2020, https://www.vaticannews.va/en/vatican-city/news/2020-04/turkson-think-covid19-aftermath-to-not-be-unprepared.html.